THE DATA HARVEST

Dominic Hand is a poet and writer based in the UK. His first book, *Symbiont: 50 Sonnets* (2020), received an Eric Gregory Award in 2021. His poetry has appeared in various journals and anthologies, including *Blackbox Manifold*, *The London Magazine*, *Reliquiae*, among others. He studied English at Oxford University, where he won the Newdigate Prize for Poetry in 2017, before completing an MPhil in Criticism and Culture at Clare College, Cambridge in 2019, and is currently completing a PhD at Merton College, Oxford, where he researches ecology and technology in contemporary poetry.

Also by Dominic Hand

Symbiont: 50 Sonnets   (Veer2, 2020)

The Data Harvest

Dominic Hand

Broken Sleep Books

ISBN: 978-1-915760-26-5

Cover designed by Aaron Kent

Edited and typeset by Aaron Kent

Broken Sleep Books Ltd
Rhydwen
Talgarreg
Ceredigion
SA44 4HB

Broken Sleep Books Ltd
Fair View
St Georges Road
Cornwall
PL26 7YH

Contents

1. 'Before utility fog outnumbers...'   9

2. 'Now that coppiced digits have begun to break away...'   10

3. 'When manufactured neural networks autoencode...'   11

4. 'Disaster recoveries become machine-readable...'   12

5. 'Dynamic tessellations, whose bounding...'   13

6. 'Clickwrapping corporate shells, quicksorts...'   14

7. 'Self-organizing feature maps—once unfurled...'   15

8. 'Eclipsed by a scenery generator's...'   16

9. 'When this fisheye planetarium, which drains...'   17

10. 'As unmonitored darknets onto flash...'   18

11. 'Preobtain | a three-dimensional scan...'   19

12. 'Bringing scanners up to date with a source upgrade...'   20

13. 'Inasmuch as instruments of turbulence revolving...'   21

14. 'As some chance-based sibylline actuary...'   22

15. 'Capsized off the earth...'   23

16. 'Glass shields stacked in riot squads...'   24

17. 'With a tariff of 1.9% per unit...'   25

18. 'Go, then pause each dream's subpar...'   29

19. 'Dredged up like pearls that underscore...'   30

20. 'As stones upon a centrifugal string overspin...'   31

21. 'Traversed by sheer tomography...'   32

22. 'Reestimate how vested attrition straightaway...'   33

23. 'Fluoroscoping firethorns whose chrominance...'   34

24. 'Unevenness of evidence—rounded-off to extradite...'   35

25. 'Reprocessing a hypermorphic windstorm...'   36

26. 'Failing that flat mimicry which resinates...'   37

27. 'When a shortage of rhodopsin turned aphotic...'   38

28. 'Come away; | make figures downplay...'   39

29. 'While globalized distribution centres reconstruct...'   40

Note   41

Acknowledgements   43

Those gilded flies
That, basking in the sunshine of a court,
Fatten on its corruption? – what are they?
— The drones of the community; they feed
On the mechanic's labour: the starved hind
For them compels the stubborn glebe to yield
Its unshared harvests
— Percy Bysshe Shelley

Why shouldn't data clouds discharge as storming supermarkets?
— Hito Steyerl

1

Before utility fog outnumbers
our sensations' maladaptive
capacitance that misremembers
exploits as implosive
as the floating gates whose termination shocks exceed
with stratospheric aerosol injections shot at speed
through a blue dome of air—whose ardours of rest
stop up with silver iodide the supercells they supersede—
the sequestering capacity of every clustered forest,
defoliated leaf by leaf, drives the data harvest
of our evidence ablaze;
while, from extinguished zones of maize,
each flock of boids that sings
of sense and outward things
distorts itself with renderings
of terrains bitmaps denature,
moving about in worlds not yet acclimatized
to positive feedback loops overturning the temperature
of disequilibrated seasons—once standardized,
now forced to make recalibrations
in line with vast deglaciations
leaving nothing to rebound the rays
that are yet the thermographic fountain of our days—
as dynamic simulations and predictive charts remodelling
fresh water cycles, which source codes overtake
with fast-flowing downrushes of information levelling
migratory tributaries and flyways in their wake,
from a central timeserver
orchestrate a changeover
cladding spent stems and oiled springs with zircaloy—
proportioned to the pattern recognitions they deploy
no blizzard can abolish or destroy—
when, upstream, the synchronizations of a river
with a totalized reality
branch out and break up the surface of the sea
that—while cultivations wither
under mechanical corruptions of uncalm weather—
eutrophies red tides and spring blooms rolling evermore
along the future desolations of an undegrading shore.

2

Now that coppiced digits have begun to break away,
            rolling cataracts across our corneas replay
self-activated flashbacks—antedated from tomorrow—
                        emerging chrome yellow
into seasonless decay. Ambiophonic, yet fulgently unclear
        in the factory-tinted anamorphic eyewear
        our high-wired datagloves fail to fully bear,
the chameleon hashes of a mipmapped butterfly
        sidestep limbic objects as they superimpose
            splines upon a swidden plane, to misdiagnose
        arborescences that hidden permutations codify,
having repurposed change and imitation to accrue
        a doubly-linked list of tropes that misconstrue
misnomered forms against our infoscapes, whose mood
                        quantizes the likelihood
            of spliced connotations falling through
a limitlessly disaffected field of view.

3

When manufactured neural networks autoencode
                    intelligence explosions to the cognate extent
                    of a virtual actor's entanglement
          in our primary lifecycles' stages gone multimode,
          the boundary layers of a mirror world shadowed
                              by globally-illuminated graticules
                              shiver apart like solar granules,
as gravitational slingshots of voyagers augment
                              a fulldome's vergeless perimeter
                              mental images re-enter
like landing lights in freefall through a digital infinity
          recursively colliding with its dark reality.

4

Disaster recoveries become machine-readable
by marking up the unintended consequence
of stranded assets thrown down on a shake table
or payloads poised upon reusable launch sites.
Destructible environments, pocked with crumple zones,
get swiped off the map as they incur the pseudorandom
precision of predator drones
razing degrees of freedom.
Digital puppetry—
making somatosensory commotion quiesce
in step with the odometry
of truck platoons gone driverless—
dissimulates its metaheuristics overturning
jussive moods with a voice command device's deep learning.
Setting whole genomes in sequence,
superintelligence
concentrates unstable factions,
matching their fusion reaction's
nameplate capacity
to triple figure-zettabytes
keeping pace with our brainstorms' neuroplasticity.

5

Dynamic tessellations, whose bounding volumes drawn
through the thresholds of a counterfactual program—
             executed as a figurehead's
             post-vitruvian
             bind pose
             throws
             anti-circadian
      frenzied zeitgebers in its stead—
mock up with a superscalar connectogram
each stage where, breaking character, avatars respawn.

Once end effectors animate through inverse kinematics
human armatures—which softlock in a labyrinth
             their perfected movements' secrets—
             from a brute-force search's
             laser-cut
             gamut
             spot welding torches
      synced to stretch-wrapping spinnerets
automate batch production systems to the nth
degree of an uncrewed probe's space-tethered acrobatics.

In a prisoner's cinema, prisoner's dilemmas run rife
when they visualize every doom-looped iteration
             of survival games—unforeseen
             by customer engagement
             chatbots'
             blind spots—
      while continual improvement
      of a ghost-manned oracle machine
pins down each quantized self's implantable location,
bought off with basic services exchanged for its pattern-of-life.

6

Clickwrapping corporate shells, quicksorts learn to rank
    silicon clients with infinity pools,
      who cut flotation costs, in flotation tanks,
      of editing silicone with mudbox sculpting tools.
Extracting obscure facial features out of greebles
    to clip them from the image planes
    of a monopsonic swimlane's
        filter bubble,
                data moats reconfigure
                with a distributed ledger
           high-yield investments in blockchain.
    Reversing ciphertext to make it plain,
     every seamlessly integrated deepfake
    of resurrected icons unmakes
  with hardly dissembled veracity
        real life's duplicity,
        to self-replicate its memes
     through connectionist deep dreams
where recessional time reworks—
in vicious cycles—our ecumene's
generative adversarial networks.

7

Self-organizing feature maps—once unfurled
        over etchplains and fjords—unobservedly blot
the abscissa and ordinate of a former world
                with a multivariate plot
           culling frustrums to remove
metasequoias outside their octrees' grove;

as, with actinoform voxels blueprinting the sky,
        cruise-controlled shock-and-awe air defences—
from a fifty-thousand-foot view—quantify
              our axons' multisense
           action potentials as their minuend;
paraesthesial losses an acceptable godsend

for anti-patterned weighted sum models to devise
        a shortest path possible to inflate the worth
of tertiary recoveries, and undecarbonize
              a future-proof earth's
        black swans as prone
as our eyes beneath a photodissociated ozone.

8

Eclipsed by a scenery generator's
predictively modelled heat island's obsidian
horizon,
offshore, where future ancestors
saddle with tipping points every diluvian
citizen

storm-chasing a runaway monsoon
with autonomous mesonets, disruptive innovations
outmode
thermohaline shutdowns to fine-tune
the cryosphere's albedo with a rollback application's
god mode

or cleanse vertical farms with ultraviolet,
as water-oxidizing catalysts turn fuel cells artificially
photosynthetic
to power bullet trains on autopilot
streamlined to regauge a kingfisher's beak as imperially
cybernetic,

when, phasing out smog blanket vapours,
rolling blackouts of smart grids shed loads overstraining
in quarantine
for some de-extinct world far from ours
where scrub towers capturing carbon go on predeveloping
a novacene.

9

When this fisheye planetarium, which drains the unilateral dark,
         demotes each motored zone to an involuntary park
re-enclosed beneath the sign of its biomorphic trademark,

         with their risk-averse protections indefectibly severe,
wireless tremors shuttle down the untapped asthenosphere
     where relics of the sunken day—deposited from anywhere—

unpick their abandoned particles. Astray in a metagalaxy,
         such multiplex arrangements stay stochastically unfree
to flare up like a flock within a katabatic wind; by proxy

                emergent properties of ant mills growing infinite
leak through multiplayer persistent state worlds to evaporate
     in holographic cloud forests, hollowed out by searchlight.

On the flipside of this flight simulation—through these readymade
         smart glasses buffered by the sun's invasive aubade—
pandistributed glidepads tip their scales and cells to intergrade

             intrinsic chronotypes with each peripheral device
in need of an adaptor for modems to decentralize
         filamentous texture maps stamped with microgravities.

10

As unmonitored darknets onto flash storage download
　　　　　　　expansion packs that supplement
　　　　　　　in-the-flesh moments
　　　　　　　with an embodied agent
recirculating timestamped deeds about each deep-tiered node,

backed up where penetration tests left off and factory resets
　　　　　　　wiped out whole factions
　　　　　　　of proprioception,
　　　　　　　multiscopic incarnations—
rigging android joint constraints from points on handheld tablets—

deinterlace an operating system's nested lattice
　　　　　　　of trojans and microbes
　　　　　　　to concatenate the globe's
　　　　　　　photon-mapping strobes
reopening in boxplots the subsets of their limbic-twinned prosthesis.

11

Preobtain
a three-dimensional scan
surmounting subterranean
repositories of spent rods catacombed within a mountain,
then synthesize with distance fog trade winds between subtropics—
antialiasing woodlands to their grains' anisotropic
texture elements—for a barycentric particle system
to make elliptical each binary star's two-body problem.

Anchor any
standpoint to its hyperlink
web-scraping spiderbots outthink—
conducting signals through moniliform and monopole antennae—
or pair the charges stress-induced in piezoelectric
sugar crystals with electrograms' anthropometric
fibrillations, as tactical immersions overkill
whole-body interactions with an omnidirectional treadmill.

Zero-sum
the imitation game
artificial neurons reframe—
parroting our trial-and-error deductions with a checksum—
as feedback-strengthened geophones' groundbreaking mechatronics
size up foreshocked subduction zones of tarmacked plate tectonics,
kriging return periods while orders of approximation
parameterize meridians with their circumnavigation.

12

Bringing scanners up to date with a source upgrade
    turns scalable the atlas
      of vertical malls humming inside a blind arcade
    where crowd simulations leave civilians as bodiless
as a man-made glass structure
whose occupancy sensors automatically
    normalize the curvature
of mirror neurons snared in an uncanny valley.

Shadow profiles netted from their end users' contacts
    paper over a mind-hive
      with lossy compressions and digital artifacts
    burned into the aisles of its time-capsuled archive,
while a crisper interface
edits defects out of each designer cryobank
    and a memory palace
topples vivid loci with a universal blank.

Far-ranging failovers geoplexing server farms
    tirelessly overclock
      the stigmergy of starlings with robotic swarms
    shepherding migrations away from every aftershock
tuned mass dampers uninstall,
as rising tides escalate the autocorrection
    of an adaptive seawall
replenishing the beach from its impure ablution.

13

Inasmuch as instruments of turbulence revolving
override full runs with their lost traction,
                supply chains exhaust
                benchmarks to adjust
                fuel cells that stall
        when they jumpstart. Still,
            before time—earthmoving
        past each de-treed spoil at speed—
deciduous forerunners deindustrialize instead
azoic island clusters with raw draglines interleaving
        plastic-eating enzymes
        to their aquamarines.

    Claytronics striving
            for the world's negation
                regenerate entirely
        from dust motes falling squarely
                over cells and waveforms, unrecorded,
which subsisted then, and no more maintain
                the unsimulated strain
of disintegrations recomposed as helixes safeguarded.

    Trigger and consequence charged as vital,
            coil-sprung with vorticity—
            like magnetic sails thrown
        by the drag coefficients
        of some echeloned device—
                    microelements,
                    near-reft of ice,
        substitute their touchstones
        for touchscreens marking the crystallinity
        of black tides stained as digital.

14

As some chance-based sibylline actuary
puts decision trees in place to maim
polymorphic underpinnings—altered by the same
crescive impulse, aimed with the inevitability
of multiclass perceptrons thrown forward to reclaim
bioinformation out of cytotoxicity
fraught with self-enveloping autolysis—
denaturants backpropagate themselves into the blue
more omissive than a desubmerged oasis
for each tegument to viralize its blotted residue
decorrelating regions of vicariance, off cue
with the other's coexistences in tow;
yet for heatstruck glaciations, liquid state machines somehow
regenerate from their global distillation's afterglow
presequenced by a sensorineural megawatt
drawing rein from stormclouds—buffered off and on
by a polar expiration's macrocyclic antiphon,
hypercatalectically outdistancing the overwrought
intermodulations hammered down each micron-
scaled conduit, bound towards a cognizant expansion slot—
whose turbulences, thickening in catalytic rings,
open out through portal sites to nowhere
where helitacks make heatwaves' thermal profilings
doomscroll down the anticommons' tragic disrepair
gamethrown by regime shifts inoperable as vapourware,
while the scope creep of duplexed interoperability
lets slide the season creep and sub-replacement fertility
of conurbations zoned off by a fintech-domed city.

15

       Capsized off the earth
as thermions accelerate, breaking through the isothere
each metronomic eyeline mimics with its trochlear
intersections wiredrawn in hybridized rebirth,
       a dielectric crosstree—
       protocolled to oversee
multichannel visions whose hypnotic antiglare
disentangles meshworked deadlocks rewoven threadbare—
       overrides the dusk where emissivities expire.

       As if padlocked by a firewall,
troubleshooting thumbnails to install a haptic gateway
in the course of every lifeworld-crashing intraday—
and quickly make that, which was nothing, all—
       a waterfall backtracks to blear
       rain sounds scrolling near
through a veil of fermions, whose licensed counterflow
fuses fulgurations with a speed ramp's ultraslow
       instant replays, humanized by datasets aglow.

       From a cauterized cocoon
within a polymeric dune—outsized by its interstitial biosphere—
dendroidal transfer modes, remaindered anywhere,
accelerate along each plesiochronous lagoon;
       before an immaterial headwind
       crystallizes to rescind
geothermal fracture lines, unnumbered underneath
skeletal quaternions that subdivide the earth
       to propagate one metaverse and haste the other's death.

16

Glass shields stacked in riot squads
    still parry us; the glidepath
of predacity marauds
    our foregrounded aftermath

along geodesic tripwires
    where the impacts of a trident
trigger wildfires
    as ignitabilities grow ambient

in overdrive; probes overlook
    conative habitats, now gone
amok like a chinook
    amid an unchained mesocyclone,

decommissioning a dustheap
    to filter out the populace,
as pandemics overleap
    the panaceas they displace

with cryogenics at remove,
    while algal blooms impede
reactor shrouds to turtledove
    spent territories they retrocede;

so lustral uptakes troubleshoot
    trace fossils from the tar
whose glyptic intervals reboot
    the perennated, wasteful gear

which fractionates an overflow
    of unexploited scree
for earthquakes to foreshadow
    every cultivated entity

with swansong, merging slipshod
    multiversities beneath
the lifting of each transferred mood
    with shock-absorbing breath.

17

With a tariff of 1.9% per unit
    200 centimetres of annual rainfall
delineate the character of a cryolite deposit
    punching holes in the departmental firewall

as the foam core of a personal flotation device
    provides 52.5% of the region's hydropower
losing 152 cubic kilometres of ice
    at a flow rate of 20,000 kilomoles per hour

doubling the rates of atmospheric CH^4
    across 12.5% of formerly protected areas
dismantling into basalt on the ocean floor
    buried with hundreds of engraved souvenirs

as eigenvalues >1 are chosen for ideal
    bitwise operations whose feature extraction
of fracture plates constructed from vanadium steel
    or copper cathodes placed in an electrolyte solution

loses 6,520 teragrams in the long term
    as the mining installations of 53 countries
increase the optimal leverage of a firm
    searching for order in a barometric series

analyzed tenfold over 140 coordinates
    to evaluate a reference dose of atrazine
when 31% of 9,600 invertebrates
    emerge heterozygous for a recessive lethal gene

and the 4-lobed calyx of a turpentine broom
    held in position by 2 external magnets
expanding by roughly 26% in volume
    parallels the bycatch caught in the dragnets

made of filaments of nylon barely 50 decitex
    strung out like a web inside a spider's nervous system
as mature rubber trees exuding 0.1 litres of latex
    with a negligible rise for every millirem

blur across intervals driving 80 mph
        through the ancestral habitat of an Iberian wolf
cleared for 173,000 terawatts of solar power
        harnessed from the rays that strike off every roof

when the density of closely separated stars
        configured by branch points on cross-sectional diagrams
with 4mb intervals between their isobars
        and an observable mass of 1.5×10^{53} kilograms

begins with an amplified redshift and ends
        in a heliosheath 40 AU from the sun
before the thermal velocity of a bow shock bends
        the ground state of an unperturbed system

where meteorite fragments found at depths of 9 metres
        amass along a track running 30 kilometres north
through each cornea decreasing by ~32 dioptres
        to magnify the hexagonal eyes of a moth

with a 5% decline the species distribution
        of the 79 organs making up a single body
exceeding the full moon with its light pollution
        infecting all the samples from a panel study

observed from a magnitude of 10 parsecs
        as clumps of red mangroves 15 metres across
with elliptical graben-like sinks at their apex
        make up 35% of the estimated loss

of 594 orthologous genes
        for any real θ between 0 and 2π
containing 1023 various proteins
        beneath the CMB cold spot in the microwave sky

as icosahedral capsids 400 nanometres wide
        represented by a union of line segments
cover 51% of the distance in a stride
        with a terminal web of actin microfilaments

because the spill contains 2 isomers of MCHM
 and the scaling exponent of 3/8 for all mammals
designed to spin at 35,000 rpm
 hits its upper limit strength of 60 megapascals

following implosions of compressed baryonic matter
 whose 80 megakelvins in an intracluster medium
contaminate the readings recorded on a light meter
 frozen in place by a tank of liquid helium

when with 79 years of rainforest left
 an alarm control unit set at 500 ohms
picks up 46 decibels from a great hornbill's nest
 along with 250,000 species still to be confirmed

as the total national output of 600,000 tonnes
 of palm oil saponified into high-lather soap
makes up just a fraction of the negative returns
 tracing the effects of a ^{14}C isotope

among dense strands of cattail and invasive macrophytes
 which build up roughly 40 PSI to inflate
the pH of the soil at 13 colliery spoil sites
 leading to a higher resting pulse rate

like a laser show scattering a continuous wave
 along a 200-mile aqueduct bringing water to the city
with the twisted perspectives of a hand-painted cave
 whose 57,000-person seated capacity

creates 200 kilocalories per mole of combustion
 so the growth of chlor-alkali as a proven technology
precipitates a rise in the rates of exhaustion
 reported by those in the packaging industry

when the length of a thousand worker ants in human terms
 equals 258 hectares of tall grass prairie
assembled into 70 trays per minute by the arms
 of a blister pack machine inspecting the quality

of silver peaches cloned from an enhanced genotype
      with a torque of 84 Nm placed in the lowest gear
causing chill damage to tissue frozen when unripe
      losing energy in storage at >1% a year

170 times faster than the Holocene baseline
      whose mosaics of sawgrass laced with open-water sloughs
shift by 473 inches at 60 frames per second
      until 97% of the area has been burned

as a t test statistic for strontium-90 activity
      gives a reading of 28,000 becquerels
in milk samples taken from farms in the vicinity
      of a pressurized graphite receptor which parallels

per human head 1,056 pounds of cement
      forming 25 million kilometres of newly paved roads
with a yearly increase of 4.6%
      across boreal regions spanning 11 different time zones

where each product review or business transaction
      accounts for ~80% of internet traffic
with an average fuel intake of 6 miles per gallon
      and an efficiency of 64% for transpacific

unmanned aerial vehicles forcing airspaces to close
      as 25.5% chance of a landslide
links up the statistics which superimpose
      16 zettabytes of data worldwide

over fluctuating spaces made of quantum foam
      where meaningful zeroes on an ordinal scale
form ∞-shaped holding patterns above an aerodrome
      like the logarithmic spirals of a chameleon's tail

dwarfing the members of a genus of wild
      steel-frame T joists reaching 60 feet in height
with 55 million rubber tyres compiled
      to fill the size of the Sahara with panels of light.

18

Go, then pause each dream's subpar
                   precircumstance whose costs outshoot
your free hand with a steel polestar,
            gearing up to plug the route
where single-use white goods impounding
        breathing rooms in taskbars pending
               type
              what hype
floats the dross on every holotype.

In profile, all your backlogged habits
                track you down, then scrape the basis
underneath which spring submits
            skewed kernels to kurtosis;
still none of this, when validating
             asset models recreating
             solid air
                from software,
can tell where your eigenfaces are.

While their hidden lives survive your own
              through interfaces making dents
in caches amortized on loan
          from ransomware investments,
every public chain that fails to stop
            has factored in your drag and drop
             indifference
              to permanence,
refreshed in mined translucence.

19

Dredged up like pearls that underscore
                    a terabyte's abyssal zone—
          immersed beneath a crypt's trap door—
                    self-sponsored presets answer for
          planned obsolescence, undergone

               while blowtorched fireflies' scattershot
concealments mould their streamline
          minds about each dormant hotspot
                    hypermetric strokes unknot
          with parabens disrupting endocrine;

               as, trammelled by conflicts of agency—
                    whose volant unions overshadow
the unleaded, rigged translucency
                    of a fountainhead technocracy—
          dark pools of arbitrage, frictionlessly, flow.

20

As stones upon a centrifugal string overspin,
multipartite viruses whirl within a mainframe,
    misrendering satin for sarin
    mists from the endgame
    locusts begin.
        Quaternary debris—
    transfumed for gasoline—
fills each storage system with the viscoelasticity
of shock absorbers, frictionlessly dampened to sideline
nonstop superfluxes with an anthropoid nonentity.

In the wake of hypercatalectic turbulence, hereinbefore
overstepped by draglines from an undeciphered filename—
    now lost like a rotifer inside a ctenophore's
    tripwired nerve-net, aflame
        at the core—
    a looped square's command key
    reels in the day to irreversibly excise
private connections with the anonymity
of lights-out warehouses that ausform and itemize
forklifts as they hinge on disimpassioned productivity.

21

Traversed by sheer tomography
branching off each radix tree—
  as rasterized abrasions on a lodestone
  dissociate the synergies they clone—
geomorphic resonances oscillate to save
 advections in a machinated sine wave;

while lenticular arrays upscale
  every immaterial detail—
   interdigitating micropulsations to engage
    coagencies that broaden as they gauge
  a marl of lithic fragments, accreting in a landmass
turned back against itself to form a wall of plexiglass—

as, with overpowered rates of growth,
   a centrifugal moth
  opens up the fabric of the world like a fumarole
    emitted from an engineered wormhole
too untraceable for aeroshells to shield its heat—
expanding in diminishing returns, like a hoofbeat

subclustering accelerated particles to duplicate
   wildwood with cyanoacrylate—
  for carbon-copied footprints to homogenize
  multi-layered clades with ores that galvanize
desertifications and clearances refined
by the valence of an overloaded mind.

Reestimate how vested attrition straightaway
strangleholds to ransom with laboursaving worksheets
    all the unskilled operatives whose disinflated breaths
        lag behind the threshold of a charging bay;
how with exponential discharge a scatter plot deletes
tanked subpopulations from the ambit of its isopleths

        when nickel and naphthalene tinge the riverbeds
in the mould of an involuntary autoclave
    whose blow fill seals bind them fast—open to the aftermath
        that tailing dams and oil rigs disperse widespread
in successive ranks to saturate a hundred-year wave
    adjusting to the sea change on a microbarograph—

        while polymeric plumes, with relative entropy,
deactivate the currents of a blinded photocell,
    and heredities subsumed inside an introgressive shibboleth
        cede to the uncertainty
        coiled moieties unshell
with thanatosensitivity in place of brumal death;

before synaptic ports, left off hook, intercept oblique
        stream-ciphered messages their keysets overhear—
eavesdropping closer to the wireframed undergrowth
        where autoresponders misspeak
    through a handling system that marks the planisphere
with the ambient passbands of a hawkmoth—

        as, wired-up to wetware, such lead-ins hypostatize
the fixed action patterns their integers remove
        hyperinstantaneously, allocating multipath
    propagations, to kyanize
with corrosive sublimates each sequestrated mangrove
        ousted from the technetronic earth.

23

Fluoroscoping firethorns whose chrominance outpours
incarnadine control points turning citrine as they flood
    in real time ray-traced hours—
        whose ambience suppressed
    by aberrances shrouds
        the vertex-shaded clouds
    like a glitch within an alkahest
        or bug within a bud—
from multilevel input queues, downstream a driver flings
deterministic finite strings through index files walled
    by algorithmic outsourcings
        whose permutations spellbind
    the overlapping wellsprings
        of image planes with shortcomings
    that object codes rewind
        to derealize the world;
while centripetal servers—infolding overtime
amid deficient spiral models wildly gone amiss
    beneath the background noise
        of malware scripts and convoys
    whose chelated alloys
        impede the forged kinesis
    of an unconstructed paradigm
        fresh hyperfunctions overwrite—
monumentalize each partial function with their widespread
double-ended queue compressed inside a gigabyte,
    boosted to encloud
        shellcodes that remove
    authentications to approve
        the factors disallowed
by a doomsday clock, whose tapered seconds shroud
edaphic liquefactions with remnants of actinide
and stratify our technofossils sealed in polysulphide.

24

Unevenness of evidence—rounded-off to extradite
choice-redacted state exceptions breaches certify—
pulls apart the leaves from every splay tree's indefinite
multilaterations keystroked indigents scrape by;
staking their heuristics on an out-of-sync lightwave
skewed with prestidigitations, spelt out to stultify
self-possessions exiled to an uncharted enclave
where gimbal locks impair the mind's anthropic eye
with enhanced security, whose lack of exigence transposes
to boxes—where unallocated space compacted lies—
hypnoidal dragonflies from their hybrid metamorphoses
each texture cache or edge vector ratifies
with samples from opinion polls, whose quality control
smooths out expectations, as a leading edge dives
back through black holes where seasoned timber and coal
piece together a pseudoforest's tindered diapositives.

25

Reprocessing a hypermorphic windstorm in a breezeway,
    ribose-columned insulants recirculate their throwaway
        gyral systematics like a silkworm's multivoltine
    photocurrents instantlessly lost in petabytes,
whose large-scale integration signals sputter out of paracrine
    pathways overloaded by hotwired antisatellites
        autoloading movements through the outlets of an ingress
    virtually the same as glass unpolished in untimeliness;
while, without a sound, unmodified exsertions interlay
    corollated agencies with anaplastic underlay,
        unshaken by expropriated terms that preapprove
    contract curves per capita of leaves to decompound
vespertine transactions, timing out hereinabove,
    with disinflated single engine quotas docking stormbound;
        so equidistant registration numbers coextend
    contralateral groundspeeds, sustained to disallow
diminishing returns within a scattered subtrahend,
    multiplying seconds that recede as they foreshadow
        future values stacked along a moonlit windowsill,
    apportioned like a monogram to patently outrun
synergistic beams falling softly to a standstill,
    glasspapering the static lost behind the midnight sun.

26

Failing that flat mimicry which resinates past harvesttime
     subefficacious vineyards stained by ambuscades of birdlime,
  in forecast arabesques symplectic manifolds now overlay
     with swallow's speed glitched runnels readjusting to the jetway;
quickscoping, densely microtextured sightlines nerf to reap
     conveyorized hard capsules from their error-margined antisleep,
  which alters with the pace of every retrograded satellite
     engarlanding its skyboxes with unobstructed oversight,
to let the quicksand at random through the fibreglass fall—
     while the outputs of the open world, rendered overall
  as mere bits of junked code, from every beauty quark's abyss
     burst out through their pipelines to a flip-screened solstice—
or let the stakes of some ascending subsumable degree
     make submersible each phototoxic heat-bleached coral tree
  with a touch of biophilia—whose residuums disposed of
     in a cytopathic autoclave, or starved of air inside a glove,
protect us from red phosphorus and osmium tetroxide
     floating down to streambeds out of reservoirs declassified
  in quick successive quantiles, to spear an assembly line
     of semaphores through silicon, and turn them heterodyne—
or let the gates of a transistor snaplock index-matched identikits
     to reconstruct faux flexures from our facial composites,
  so what comes of their eidetically deputized domain
     communicates no notes beyond its dominant refrain.

When a shortage of rhodopsin turned aphotic by the morning
    having ratified its pyrotechnic draft withdrawals overnight
        hardens to crash-land against the microalloys bordering
            isolated exit lanes with backstops flooding watertight
underclasses stranded in austerely rattled underpasses
segregated further from the featherbedded few
whose custom-made immunities laundered free of trespasses
swipe along the rictus to exsanguinate its ensign blue
            caved in with the weight of undelivered strenuosities
                as underpowered choruses elect to sloganize
            soft seditious sawdust with redepleted sovereignties
              laying off their workflown engines all to palletize
landlocked queues of products bound in polyacrylamide
for a self-applauding captive global island to miscue
automatic sliding doors with linkspan ramps that redivide
stateless crowds to shore up its trickle-down revenue
                inflating import quotas with repurposed disutility
              to tamper ballpark figures with tiers that misinstall
                blanket measures bolstering the trafficability
            of foreign paper tigers every time the markets fall
disbursing golden parachutes to cut the civil wire
of economy classes drinking in the sinking feeling
of points-based push-pull factors ramped up in the crossfire
of impersonated flourished native guilds electioneering
            fields of folk who tailspin with the merited delusion
              that photomasked opposing audit firms monopolize
        with overtasked mass energy buoyed by mass expulsion
    of non-refoulements warranting dark tourists to desensitize
their sidetracked eyes to stowaways' unworkable homerun
over vantablack rogue waves that break apart corexit
oil dispersants sprayed to clean up tanker slicks per tonne
of undocumented noncompliant tax gaps lost in transit.

28

Come away;
make figures downplay
penury privatized assets upsize
until their deadweight gloss subsides,
while windfalls of profligate havens untether
subsidies scanter than air through a zither.

Come away;
your head-mounted display
will write the world out as it thumbwheels
over optimized clays, where electrical eels
jam the live feed whose spectrograms sustain
rejuvenescence drunk from a diode-lit fountain.

Come away;
the immunoassay
of antigens tracked down then lost in transmission
laterally flows into short-lived remission,
when sterilized firmaments fail to save
segregants clamouring wave after wave.

Come away;
lead trackers astray
to a walk-in boscage where blue morphos blend
their dorsal-ventral surface effects with your eyelids to upend
motion-captured silhouettes—stealthily made hollow—
dodging telemetric markers, doubling back to shadow.

Come away
from this plug-and-play
fantasia, where, out of order hurled—
fieldstripping each anthrome's remodelled lifeworld—
technical pens scrawl their ouroboric maze
on a skybox; horse latitudes bray as they stargaze.

29

While globalized distribution centres reconstruct
from a choropleth map's infographic
the gross domestic product
of barcode-classified traffic,
communication lines autodestruct
barriers to entry, once their plenum—
reverse-engineering
an internet of things—
reifies a virtuality continuum.

Direction finders bear down their ground trace,
distancing the whereabouts of grid cells
through vanishing points that deinterlace
the obsolete videotaped pixels
of abandonware, like debris in space,
shorted out, sparked blue by a hurricane's
stadium effect, whose arced power flash
transects like lightning our coronal planes
where mirex bioaccumulates
with fly ash particulates
and dichlorodiphenyltrichloroethane,
before the heart's voltage under repetitive strain
unearths such moral hazards;
as scale models kitbash
an eyewall's effects, and mental images
fizzle out beneath the technical standards
of expansion cards
whose comparative advantages—
laying waste the autoimmunities
of plagioclimax communities'
phylogenetic affinities—
transform the anomaly detection
honing our focus groups' data collection.

NOTE

The 29 sections of The Data Harvest began as adaptations of a variety of 17th and 18th-century poems. These urtexts were then modified using a vast range of terminologies and textual materials gleaned from information databases. While transformed virtually beyond recognition, the poems' structures, rhymes and metres were reverse-engineered to approximate those of their original sources.

LAY OUT YOUR DATA

Ingram Content Group UK Ltd.
Milton Keynes UK
UKHW040700060723
424652UK00006B/170